Party

Like a Lacrosse Star *

by

Paul Montgomery

Cover photo of sewer cover on Urban Street,
Title page artwork,
Map of Durham and Duke
© Paul Montgomery 2007

ISBN 978-0-6151-7150-0

First Edition

For the students

I was awoken one spring morning by the sounds of banging pots and pans.

Party Like a Lacrosse Star

As I struggled to keep sleeping and wished the sound to go away, the banging of the pots and pans, the shouts and whistles kept me from my slumber. It was 9 a.m. on a Sunday morning and I was having a rare sleep-in from my news website duties.

The sound would stop from time to time. I kept hoping it wouldn't continue but it would start up again. Eventually, I figured I should see what the commotion was about for myself. As I opened the door to my 2nd floor 4-

plex exterior metal staircase I noticed a photocopied ½ sheet of paper. On it was written something to the effect of:

> Today you will hear the banging of pots and pans. We condemn what has taken place in our community.

Not having the faintest idea what they were upset about I thought I would go take a look.

As I turned the corner I saw a group of about 20 people banging pots and pans in front of a house on Buchanan Boulevard.

In the crowd I saw the pretty Indian girl from the watershed society.* There she was yelling slogans and looking irate. What had brought her to such indignation?

After watching awhile and not really

---

* Details changed to protect person's privacy.

knowing what was happening I returned home. There, I fired up my computer. After a quick look at *The Herald-Sun*'s website I found an article about the lacrosse team being accused of a brutal gang rape. The crime sounded horrific.

However, the information online gave me pause. Although the crime was terrible no one had even been charged yet. The mob outside was enraged over a crime that had not even been proven. What would set such ire in motion with so little evidence or even official arrest?

The idea that the pretty Indian girl would partake of such a mob rush to judgment gave me a negative impression of her.

While it was not a lynch mob in the old West or, God forbid, the old South style, still it was a mob and it was quick to condemn the actions alleged to have occurred. I had never witnessed directly such wrath.

It caused me to consider the reasons for

their anger. Certainly, the crime alleged was one reason. A violent gang rape by three men after a striptease show in front of the Duke University lacrosse team in a house across the street from Duke University's East Campus. Violence against women in any form is an abomination and certainly deserves opprobrium.

However, did the fact that the accused went to Duke have anything to do with the people's hatred? That was an interesting question. Would they be so quick to condemn someone from another university, another occupation, another race? How about another class? Would these folks have been so willing to go bang pots and pans in a public housing project instead of Trinity Park (a neighborhood name in Durham)?

Maybe at this point in the story a little background is called for. Durham is a small city, around 250,000 in the city and county, and it is a city of neighborhoods. The former world's tobacco capital, the tobacco companies have all decamped for surrounding country towns and left in their place mouldering and refurbished tobacco warehouses and factories. But, they have bestowed one glory, the city's current largest employer, Duke University.

Being in a city with Duke University is somewhat like being in the UN as a country other that the US. Their power is near absolute but is best exercised in a velvet glove. However, the cultural and monetary benefits demand at least a grudging and willful respect.

Beyond Duke's power, the city itself is a white minority city with 45% white, another 45% black, and the balance-holding remainder of 10% other. When the county is added in, the balance tips more to the white side but remains a white minority county.

This balance of power translates to some vicious city council and school board debates, elections, scenes. Issues can be contentious and hard fought that might seem irrelevant to an outsider, much like family battles.

Overall, Durham is the most scorned city in North Carolina. Part of that is being a blue Democrat city in a red state. Part of that is racism about black political power in a concentrated form. Part of it is a violent gang culture that degrades the populace. Life is cheap in some parts of Durham. Woe betide you should you happen to be in the wrong part at the wrong time.

Now, with my description of Durham as a city of neighborhoods and my apartment in Trinity Park near Duke, you may have the impression that I am immune from the gang violence. Well, the neighborhoods that structure Durham do not run in straight lines or comprise well-defined sectors.

Here on the Carolina Piedmont's rolling hills and valleys, neighborhoods and property values follow the hollows. In an area with annual rainfall above 44 inches and not too infrequent hurricanes, the poorer houses are located by the creeks that crawl through the clay soils.

This can make for some wealthier homesteads being just up the hill from humbler dwellings. In Trinity Park, which has its low spots, the poorer cousin neighborhood is Walltown which lies across Buchanan Boulevard and up the street from Duke.

I rode the bus sometimes with Eugene Wall. He is an octogenarian whose father helped build Duke's East Campus wall and found Walltown.

Anyway, beyond the physical geography, you really never do know where violence might strike. Shortly after I moved to Durham in 2002 there was a drug dealer shoot-out at Northgate Mall. No one survived that standoff as both men shot each other dead. Northgate Mall is at the northern edge of both Trinity Park and Walltown just across from Club Boulevard.

The street I walk to go to Northgate

Mall is Watts Street. It is a beautiful tree-lined mansion-filled street where the shade is exquisite and the gardens well-maintained. Of course, my apartment building is there, the Harris Apartments, and other apartments and huge looming off-campus houses, the Duke equivalent of fraternities. Even here, among the gardens, shade trees, and butterflies violence can strike in an instant.

One day while walking home a black SUV took a very sharp left turn the wrong way onto one-way Watts Street. In hot pursuit were two cop cars with sirens blazing. The hot acrid smell of oil and rubber burning was thick in the air after they had passed by. My heart was in my throat, if the SUV had rolled I would have been in a dire...

Since I stopped writing this on the 22nd of December, 2006 and today on the 26th, the Durham County District Attorney Mike Nifong has dropped the rape charges against the three lacrosse team defendants: Collin Finnerty, Reade Seligmann, and David Evans, the erstwhile team captain. While this unleashed some sighs of relief, they were short-lived as everyone realized that the sexual assault and unlawful restraint charges were staying. Basically, all this means is that no penis was used in the commission of this crime. Correction, that no insertion of a penis occurred during commission of the crime. As relieving or horrific as that prospect is, the fact remains that the prosecution continues.

Where was I? Oh yes, dire circumstances made me react instinctively to jump off the sidewalk and onto an ivy-covered steeply sloping yard to avoid a car collision death had the vehicle rolled after turning onto Watts Street.

So you see violence is able to penetrate the best neighborhoods, the unlikeliest occasions, the most safe of persons.

You know, I feel like I am still misleading you as to the makeup of my neighborhood near Duke. It also houses a great number of students, some in party houses, some in apartments. And, when not in school they used to get up to some fun hi-jinks. About once a week or more often the loud music and raucous voices of youngsters enjoying themselves would echo through Trinity Park during the afternoons and evenings and nights of years past. Why the past tense and references to the past?

Well, the parties have temporarily been damped down by several factors. First among these would have to be the influence of the scheming busybodies of the Trinity Park Neighborhood Association (TPNA). Remember my reference to strong neighborhood identity. Well, the defenders of this neighborhood identity are the neighborhood associations.

Members of the Trinity Park Neighborhood Association are primarily homeowners who pay dues of $12 a year to belong. Granted, the TPNA does some great things. They put on little neighborhood parties and help host the Durham Symphony Orchestra in the spring. (A disclosure, I was formerly the general manager of the DSO.)

However, thanks to some agitations and activism, not all of it officially TPNA business, the student party scene has been quieted.

The first move in this direction was an agreement reached between the city and Duke University. This was an agreement to allow the Duke University Police Department to patrol one block into the surrounding neighborhood. In Trinity Park's case that was to Watts Street within Trinity Park. While the most oft-stated reason for this change was to provide more of a police presence in the surrounding neighborhoods, really there was not much need for increased patrols in Trinity Park because it is a relatively low crime area. The true hidden reason was to harass students and combine efforts between the Duke police and the Durham police to increase enforcement.

This backfired in a serious manner when an overzealous member of a Durham PD task force (the Alcohol Law Enforcement effort or ALE) walked into a house party to serve underage drinking citations. These were subsequently thrown out when the students had the presence of mind, as well as probably the parental advice and money, to hire an attorney to have the tickets tossed. The officer, after all, had no warrant nor any probable cause.

The second effort was an agreement between a local landlord of several student houses and Duke University with some Trinity Park midwives to have the university purchase some student houses and then to resell them to family purchasers who would presumably be quieter in the evenings.

Why these activities raise my hackles is twofold. First, these kids are primarily good kids. They drink beer, they shout and yell, they dance, they blast loud music, they slam their car doors as they come or leave for this or that party. Which of us did not do some similar things when we were young? The majority of these, with the exception of drinking beer if you are under 21, are not crimes.

(The 21-year-old drinking age is one of Ronald Reagan's least government reductionist legacies. Born of a desire to create uniformity of drinking ages among the large population, close geographically Eastern states, the 21-year-old drinking age was blackmailed through to the states by the threat of withheld highway funding. This consequent loss of rights was the freedom-loving president's gift to young adults of the previous 25 years.

The all-too-obvious result is that young drinkers are driven from the store and the bar to the back alley bootlegger, the house party, and the street; and, when the party gets busted by the police – into cars and taxicabs.)

A few unusual incidents stick out in my mind. Guys streaking in the distance. Girls using my station wagon to brace themselves as they took pisses in my parking lot. Of course, these do stick out because they are unusual and this, over the course of 4½ school years.

And, the most unusual of all. One late night on a parent visitation weekend I heard some loud shouts. They were more intent and harsher than usual. Looking out my 2nd floor window surveying Urban Street an extremely drunken father and son were shouting at each other. The son was continually imploring the father, "I want you to be a part of my life."

The father responding with equal urgency, "I thought I already was." From this point of seeming agreement, the pair grew increasingly belligerent, eventually coming to blows. Obviously, there was some fundamental disagreement that lay unexpressed. As I watched them wrestle on my apartment's lawn I considered calling the police. However, I judged that in this spasm of violence, perhaps they might come to a state of respect that their words or past were keeping them from.

Eventually, the police did arrive and they quickly separated the combatants. The father going off to get picked up by a cab, the son retreating to a house next door, the chance for a battle-induced comity passed. Yes, violence can be here, too.

But, for the most part the students would party and frolic, make a lot of noise, drink and yell, maybe the occasional fight.

The second reason the police crackdown upset me was because the Trinity Park homeowner's moved into this neighborhood near the university with the full knowledge that they were moving into a student district. These folks knew what to expect when they arrived. Now, it seems like they want all the advantages of homeownership near a great university without the hardship of actually having to deal with the students. This seems like a situation that is unlikely to ever exist, no matter the police presence.

When the crackdown was in the works there were efforts by students and citizens to come together in a positive manner. A reporter from *The Chronicle*, the Duke student paper came by. I filled his ears with some of the stuff written above but ended up being quoted about being young once and having fun then.

Around the same time a Duke student came by to let the neighbors know about a block party. I gave him an earful about how I like the kids and think I told him that its nice to get invited to a party once and awhile. There had been a party where women wrestled in KY jelly in bikinis. That party took place next door to my place and I had to read about it in the newspaper. I think a courtesy invite is at least called for under those circumstances. Police apparently broke up that party sending bikini-clad KY-laden nubiles scrambling through the neighborhood. Again, missed it.

He took my point and invited me to their block party. As I drove home the day of the party I saw them decorating shade trees near the street and setting up sawhorse tables. Although invited I thought I would leave them to it. After all, youth is a country you pass through but once and is best visited for short times thereafter.

I feel like I've gone far afield from my original topic. This whole discussion of Durham and my neighborhood was simply to give you some background. What was the cause of the ire?

Perhaps it was those darn students. All I know is that it soon became intense. The media rained down on my once peaceful corner, drunk on tales of sex crimes and town-gown strained relations, multi-racial crime in a multi-racial city. It had all the ingredients to go national. And the insatiable maw must be fed and it has a daily appetite for other's misery.

Before long the local and national media were doing stand-ups in front of "the lacrosse rape house" as I took to calling it.

That 1st week after the pots and pans was the craziest, with events culminating for me at the Take Back the Night march from East Campus to Duke Chapel. As I was out taking a walk I saw some of the media madness happening at the house. News crews, reporters, and satellite trucks were converging to capture the excitement.

After shopping at the Durham Food Co-op and returning up Buchanan Blvd. I was stopped by Allen Breed, AP reporter. I gave him some of the background shared here. I ended up being quoted for an article that went out on the wire a little later. In the article I am quoted as saying that there was a rush to condemn the lacrosse players perhaps because they were people of privilege. I also said that there was more than met the eye in this case, that there were hidden depths.

The reason I felt that there were hidden depths to this case, and here I need to rely on memory of how I felt and thought at that time, so as to provide an accurate record, is that the story of how it happened did not make any logical sense to me. Given the timeline in play at that time, the stripper would have had to be pulled from her dance, been raped, & then left.

Having been to a few ecdysiacal exhibitions in my time I know a little bit about the behavior of males in such a situation. If a stripper begins a dance and then suddenly stops, in a beer-fueled crowd of rowdy lacrosse players, those guys are going to go nuts. The idea that hopped up stripper tricks are going to allow anything to occur before a full show has gone on is absurd. Those guys would be foaming and frothing at the mouth ready for their glimpse of female pulchritude.

So, something did not seem right from the very beginning. And there were other discrepancies. The original 911 calls described someone being called racial epithets. However, the calls variously described the callers as driving by, stopped, and standing in front of the house. Besides, who calls 911 about being called a racial epithet? Is that really a police matter? Or, is that someone looking to bring in a police presence? To my knowledge, the caller has never been identified.

When the police arrived, the house was deserted. Factor in the tenuous relationship between the Duke students and the police that existed then, and it is no wonder, a 911 call made, police presence threatened, best to vacate the scene than deal with the cops, at the least underage drinking violations and the worst...who knows?

Uh oh! Breaking news - The North Carolina State Bar has filed ethics charges against Durham County District Attorney Mike Nifong. The charges primarily deal with the extensive comments Mr. Nifong made regarding the case to the media. The charges specify the possibility that the comments created public outrage impeding the chance for the defendants to receive a fair trial. So, the state bar has officially charged Mike Nifong for the outrage.

However, a lit match dropped in a bucket of water sizzles out immediately. If Mike Nifong did strike a spark, it found its fuel.

I feel I must admit to my biases and actions in relation to Mr. Nifong. Frankly, I think he bungled this case for reasons previously considered and the obvious state bar censures.

I voted for Mr. Nifong's opponent in the Democratic primary. Mr. Nifong won with 45% of the vote. And, I both signed and solicited signatures for a petition to put Durham County Commissioner Lewis Cheek on the ballot in the general election. Mr. Nifong won again with another underwhelming 48% of the vote.

So, as much as I think Mr. Nifong was generally incompetent in his handling of the Duke lacrosse case I still think we need to look beyond him and his statements about "hooligans" to find the real reasons for the outrage that day. Mr. Nifong cannot be understood outside his environment.

So, a word or two about my imagined reasons for Mr. Nifong's actions. It is possible that he felt he needed to crack down on Duke students, much like the police enforcement had been stepped up. Or, maybe he wanted to strike back after the embarrassments of losing on the convictions of the students for underage drinking. Or, was there some general dyspepsia related to Duke? Anyway, that is about all I can come up with.

Another news flash - A district attorney association in North Carolina has asked D.A.

Mike Nifong to remove himself from the case. I don't have much to say on that matter except that I agree with them.

You know, something that has escaped my analysis thus far is Duke's behavior and culpability. When I left home this morning another former student house was being refurbished for a new family. That made me think that Duke bears a huge degree of responsibility for this mess. Not because they have allowed students to run wild, quite the contrary. They condoned the crackdown. They seem to want the Trinity Park ideal of a university without students. They purchased the Trinity Park homes that are being reconditioned for families. They jettisoned the coach of the lacrosse team when it became uncomfortable to allow him to remain with Duke any longer. This, because his kids were condemned without proof. Granted, as an excuse they used the canard that his players had an excessive number of alcohol violations. This was a direct result of Duke's own stepped-up police enforcement.

On my way home I typically pass the corner of Buchanan Blvd. and Chapel Hill Street. Located on this corner is the Emily Kryzewski Family LIFE Center. Coach K helped build this community center to honor his mother and provide a play place for young basketballers. One evening recently on my way home from my job with UNC (That's right, I work for UNC but live half a block from Duke. Duke has a near impenetrable human resources department. As Durham's largest employer, I have yet to score an interview.) I saw a prostitute on the corner. (I'm not completely sure it was a real prostitute. It could have been a cop.) She tried to catch my eye and waggled her voluminous bosoms at me and said something like, "How about it?" to which I said no. Anyway, one day I was passing this very corner when I heard an interview with Coach K. He said he remained friends with the lacrosse coach and he made a none-too-veiled threat that if Duke ever tried to throw him overboard in a similar ignominious manner that they would rue the day.

This is a very interesting example of a double standard that is on display. If the lacrosse players had been basketball players, Coach K would never have been fired. The response from Duke would have been entirely different. I saw Coach K on *Charlie Rose* the other night. When asked about the Duke lacrosse scandal he said it was a story of the outside world trying to impose its story on Duke and Durham. Charlie went weak on him and didn't press it any further. Of course, Coach K is the franchise for Duke basketball. He is virtually untouchable and he can write books on leadership and avoid questions on *Charlie Rose* about his star player J.J. Redick being arrested for DUI after the season ends.

Coach K wrote the book with his daughter. She echoed his answer on *Charlie Rose* that this was an outside problem that was imposed on Durham. While this isn't patently false, it is an answer worthy of a public relations weasel and not a responsibility-taking coach and daughter teaching us all how to be ethical leaders.

I must confess to a dislike of Coach K. While most of this is of the harmless, hated rival variety, there was a particular incident that set me against Coach K and Duke. While I could recount it here, let me go back to a screed I wrote at the time when I was still steaming over the occurrence.

I was sooo pissed off Saturday night. I am practically still recovering from the anger, humiliation, idiocy, shame, and disgust.

What could someone have

done to make me so enraged? Why would I care so much in the first place?

My daughter received a couple of tickets for the 2003 Duke Basketball Banquet. She got these tickets for partaking in a reading program sponsored by the Duke Men's Basketball program.

Here in Durham there is a religion. It is men's college basketball. There is a high priest and his name is Mike Kryskeoprststrawejljaksdasi (pronounced Shuh - Chef - Ski). There is a goddess and her name is Nannerl Keohane.

Frankly, I am scared to write such negative things about the largest employer in town, not to mention the only one worth praying to. Damn, did I leave out how pissed off some Bible Belters are going to be reading those last few sentences. Anyway, here goes.

So, we get some tickets to a BANQUET! How did I know it was a BANQUET! It said so on the tickets. It said so three times. BANQUET! BANQUET! BANQUET!

So, my daughter and I get dressed up. Or, stayed dressed up in my case. Don't eat dinner. Because...we are going to a BANQUET!

The first hint that things were amiss was when we arrived no one seemed to care about taking our tickets. Now, these tickets had a face value of $15.00. Obviously, this value was not correct in the slightest.

People generally don't care about taking tickets when the tickets are worthless. In some cases, this is because they have many more seats than will be filled by patrons so they are trying to fill the house so as not to disappoint the performers.

You know, I don't care about how many times I have used the word so. This is a rant and demands a little informality.

So, here we were dressed up and hungry. Now, to try and disprove my idiocy. I know it may not be possible. I do not believe I was the only dressed up and hungry and pissed off parent there that night.

I saw them. I heard them. They were there.

(What isn't evident in that fragment was that for participating in the reading program my daughter had been promised those banquet tickets for herself and an adult. So, we had had quite a while to whet our appetites. Perhaps, it was common knowledge that these banquet tickets were actually not for the banquet but for seats in the stands after the banquet attendees had had their entrees on the stadium floor.

It really sucked to arrive hungry and to get super pissed off seeing people eating on the stadium floor while we were in the stands. No, no concessions were open even. They just paraded the basketballers around with a corresponding light show.

This program was part of their outreach to the community. They were promoting reading to neighborhood schools. My daughter's school did not participate the next year, possibly because of the disappointment of the unlived-up-to hype.)

As silly and hurt as that is, it is a good example of the kind of lumbering lunkhead of a giant presence Duke can be in Durham. For them to deny their impact and claim to be blameless is nothing short of shameful. Of course, the only ones peddling the blamelessness story are Coach K and his daughter. The rest of Duke has decided to go on the attack sensing Mr. Nifong's weakness and the case's wobbling foundation.

Wow, I've so confused myself that I don't know where to rejoin the story. How about during that crazy week after the incident of condemnation with the pots and pans? Shortly after having given my thoughts to Allen Breed I took part in a Take Back the Night march. Mr. Breed had tipped me off to it. I must say I was a little drawn to the spectacle of it all.

There, in front of the student union were organizers and speakers for the Take Back the Night march. I had wanted to take part in one for awhile anyway. Marching would not be so bad for me and may do some good for others. Besides, I had been touched by rape in my life. Two girlfriends of mine had been raped in the past. Many men are touched by rape and sexual violence, oftentimes because the women they loved have been hurt.

Another news flash - Duke is allowing two of the students, Collin Finnerty and Reade Seligmann to re-enroll. Duke obviously thinks the charges will come to nothing. However, this magnanimity, with charges still pending, is in stark contrast to their behavior when the charges were first announced. What has changed in the mean time is people's confidence in Mike Nifong and the strength of his case.

But, doesn't Duke need to maintain a consistency of behavior, charges then = charges now, even though actual rape charges have been dropped, or is this ad hoc relaxing of standards warranted by their ad hoc expulsions. I think it did have to do with felony charges pending. But, weren't they always innocent until proven guilty. Perhaps, not in Duke's eyes, at least, while they were a liability.

You know, this raises the important issue that Duke did not fight for these students or their coach in the beginning. The administration was quite happy to watch them twist in the wind until their resignation/expulsions were inevitable. This was consistent with their anti-student approach displayed during the police crackdown. Someone was giving the wink and the nod to the enforcement authorities as they were putting the smackdown on student frivolity. This hard-ass approach was a natural extension. When the late night knock on the door came for these students, the Duke administration pointed the way for Mike

Nifong to take them out.

A little perspective, this crisis came in the first year of Richard Brodhead's presidency at Duke. He had faced another crisis early in his hiring when Coach K was flirting with becoming coach of the professional team, the L.A. Lakers. In that case, Brodhead had to be seen as bending over backwards for his athletic star. Shudder. What would Duke do without its celebricoach? I'm sure the forcing of his resignation was never in the cards for this Duke coach.

But, back to the Take Back the Night march. There we were in front of the Student Union. Before too long a married couple and their child, friends of mine, showed up. We had met spontaneously like this before when crosses had been burned in Durham. That time it was a candlelit vigil. This time a march. Both were what I felt to be an obligation of all citizens who needed to represent themselves for a tolerant and non-violent society. The TV cameras glared, Allen Breed made his way through the crowd getting statements. Soon enough, it was time for the march to begin. Somehow, I was on the far left of the crowd. The parade started from that direction. "Have you ever felt like you were leading the parade?" I said to my friends as we took first position behind the banner and began to yell slogans. If you review the tape of the event you'll see me in the vanguard.

After walking the distance to Duke Chapel I was taken aback by the number of satellite trucks parked around the lawn in front of Duke Chapel. By the way, Duke Chapel is a building worthy of cathedral status that is built in the Gothic style, as are the majority of the buildings on Duke's West Campus.

It is such a cliche in regard to any Southern story to have the adjectives Gothic and steamy appear. In this case, Durham and Duke have the Gothic for real and the humidity to match.

News flash - A Duke student has decided to sue his professor over a failing grade. The student was a lacrosse player and claims he was passing the course until the lacrosse incident occurred. Then, he was failed, he feels, as a result of the professor's anti-lacrosse player bias. This reminds me of an interview from that first crazy week. I believe it was on the WUNC radio station show *The State of Things.* They were speaking with a Duke professor. I thought it was crazy ridiculous how willing this guy was to condemn not only the lacrosse players but all Duke students as spoiled and irresponsible. This prof seemed to have a default setting of guilty for the Duke students. I thought at the time that this guy needs to get a new job if he can't see the good in his own students and presume them to be innocent.

Also, another news flash is the news that the accuser is to have a paternity (DNA) test for her new baby. The test is to rule out the

Duke players. But since their DNA has not shown up before this point, it probably never will.

As I was out walking on my break I thought of an event that I return to often in my thoughts about Durham. One day, while walking between where Chapel Hill St. becomes Duke University Rd. (Streets change names with great frequency in Durham.) I was crossing the street in front of the car when I heard the driver say to the passenger, "He think he better than us, cause he white." Apparently, by using the crosswalk in front of a car driven by two black people I had incurred their indignation. I was not used to this kind of latent anger in regards to race having come from the relatively monoracial state of Montana. Here was someone who became offended by my mere act of walking in front of their car. How much more angry would they be if I had really done something disrespectful?

Here was a level of anger practically incomprehensible to me as a white guy from Montana.

Back to the drama of the day of the march. No one seemed to get angry about this march taking up much of Campus Drive and blocking the cross streets. But, cop cars were in abundance and people who got stuck probably were simply wisest to turn off their motors and wait for the parade to pass by. The Take Back the Night march brought back thoughts to me of two girlfriends who had been raped. I thought that my march was for them if nothing else. Two beautiful women who never deserved such ill treatment. One had been violently raped while 14 or so, had facial reconstructive surgery (yes, that bad) and had had an abortion (always something I return to when I consider my pro-choice views). The other, had been raped while undergoing psychiatric treatment. I had seen the far smaller marches in the past and had wanted to join them to represent for my old loves.

As the march reached its conclusion at the base of Duke Chapel, the organizers called for media cooperation to respect the privacy of marchers who tell their individual stories of violence in their lives. Before they began to speak I crept away and returned home to watch TV.

As I arrived home there was a message on my machine from a lady working for the *Vinnie Politan Show* on Court TV on Sirius Satellite Radio. I returned the call and found out Allen Breed had dropped the dime that I might be a good guest. If I wanted to be on the show, they would call me at 6:15 a.m. and interview me live. I agreed and went to bed.

The phone call the next morning awoke me. In the interview I told of the outrage on display; the, what looked like, bloody toilet on the lawn of the Duke lacrosse house. How there was more than met the eye in the case. And, how the Duke kids could afford the best legal advice. Also, how little sympathy even their own profs showed towards them.

The rest of the story is well-known, a preening D.A., a failing case, a rigorous defense, Duke's willingness to wash its hands of the whole affair.

A week or two later the New Black Panthers marched to the lacrosse house. I was hearing a helicopter hovering directly over my house. I kept expecting the sound to fly off in another direction. Eventually I had to peer out of the house, there was a chopper directly overhead.

Then, the sound of marchers. There they were and chanting, "Guilty, guilty, guilty." I had to get out of town to Chapel Hill to go to work. Cars were stacking up on Urban Street already. As I drove out of town, down Watts Street, there were cop cars blocking every side street feeding to Buchanan Boulevard. I drove to Chapel Hill Street and to Duke University Road on my way to my job with UNC.

Party Like a Lacrosse Star -

The Update

It seems to me more deep background on Durham is needed. It is a deep city with all kinds of cultural undercurrents. To assume complete knowledge is ridiculous. To presume a personal focus imperative.

Let me explain a little bit about how things get done in Durham. This example is by no means inclusive but rather demonstrative. I'm loving those "ive" words lately.

Regarding the construction of a new performing arts center, I visited some public meetings on this structure, its design, funding, purpose; in my capacity as the general manager of the Durham Symphony Orchestra.

While the amount of public participation was great. The mystery of these meetings was always, "What did Duke think? What will Duke contribute?" But, Duke didn't have a representative at those meetings. So, the city reps would have to say, "Well, Duke says such-and-so. Duke thinks thus-and-so. " Then, at the next meeting it would be. "Well, Duke says so-and-so. Duke will do thus-and-so." Do you get my drift?

In other words, Duke was having its own non-public meetings that were not notified between the public meetings.

My experience in public matters is limited but Montana does have one of the strongest public meeting statutes. Would I be wrong in assuming that this activity was out of the public eye? Even if this activity involved negotiations, wouldn't this be enough of a compelling interest to require openness? North Carolina has a similar public meeting law but I don't think it is as widely enforced or respected as Montana's is.

Although, I confess to a little naiveté with regards to the workings of government, I am not immature enough to realize that this is the way things get done the world around.

There is a similar story related to the American Tobacco Complex. This group of buildings, the old factory and warehouse grounds of the American Tobacco Co., manufacturers of Lucky Strike cigarettes, sits across Blackwell Street from the new Performing Arts Center being debated in the above paragraphs. In contrast to the public input, as constrained as it was, solicited for the performing arts, the American Tobacco complex developers created an outdoor stage area and performance space on their "campus".

This development was made possible by

large ($100 million) public money inflows. So, public money set the stage for the largesse of the private sector in creating a sense of community at this now private development; a sense of community the developers can profit from and the public is excluded from providing direction to.

This reminds me of the simulation of city that is known as "The Streets of Southpoint". This is a local mall that has been fashioned to resemble downtown Durham. It has mellow music coming from fake rock speakers. It has something else, too. It has no public, it has only customers.

Here, there are no panhandlers, no shufflers, stumblebums, or wastoids. Only the financially capable who do not disturb the capitalist impulse are welcome. There is something marvelous about this. The music plays, the people smile, the customers are friendly. But, in some profound ways it is fakery. Any sense of poverty or the poor is disguised outside the gates.

If the shopping mall is our public square, it has forgotten the public.

I suppose I bring this up because there I was movin' and a-groovin' at the grassy area at American Tobacco. Rough Draft was playing some great funk hits. Here was a bright and sunny warm summer day. The grass was green and well-kept. The music great, beer was flowing. Why wasn't something like this able to be accomplished by our city? Why do the public events seem so anemic by comparison?

I guess a free market advocate would say that the government is so inept that only the private sector could throw a fun party. However, it is only the kind of party that could be thrown with mountains of public cash.

And, I felt left out. There was a great performance space, wonderful music, fun times but bereft of public input.

This wasn't the only reason I felt left out. I had ridden my bike down to the

American Tobacco. Imagine my surprise, actually I was not so surprised because I had been there before, to discover they had no bike racks. This was a direct result of the lack of public involvement.

The public component of the funding for American Tobacco consisted of large parking garages. For some reason no bike racks among all the spaces for cars. All right, so much for the public sector. How about the private? Among all the wonderments of American Tobacco there are no bike racks. Total failure for alternative transport.

And, here is the greatest irony. The American Tobacco campus is at the head, or tail if you prefer, of the American Tobacco Trail. This is a bike and pedestrian trail that is a paved over railbed running about seven miles from downtown Durham to The Streets of Southpoint mall. It winds through some great neighborhoods and kudzu-covered brush and provides an excellent ride on a nice fall or spring day.

OK, so my town's not perfect. What place is? I just want to give you an idea of what Durham is like.

All this discussion of American Tobacco makes me wonder why they left town. Perhaps, the aging physical plant; the high cost to rebuild in a central city; an older, expensive workforce; all mitigated a move to the country. However, there was a time, an earlier time, when loyalty to a city and investment in a place was considered good business and an example of corporate stewardship beyond the business factors involved.

A central city location provided easy access to a labor force that might rely on public transport or walking. Rail lines could be run to supply the needed raw materials. Now, having your workforce all drive private vehicles and having materials trucked in seems to make more business sense. The small town charities and fund-raisers present a relief to the ever-burgeoning civic needs of even a small city like Durham.

With the amount of scorn heaped on tobacco companies, perhaps a lower profile suits their public relations needs. In Durham mainly the names remain: American Tobacco, Duke, Liggett & Myers, Chesterfield, Lucky Strike, Bull Durham.

There is a great exception known as the Duke Homestead and the American Tobacco Museum. Set amidst the neighborhoods of Durham and not far from Interstate 85 is the lovely old homestead of the Duke family.

There is their first tobacco factory, a small, barn-like building with a raised wood floor. And, next door is the American Tobacco Museum. This isn't just all about American the company but incorporates all of the American tobacco landscape.

One of the best features of the history museum is a black-and-white TV that shows a series of cigarette advertisements. That, along with some classic packaging and the cigarette-rolling machine that started it all, and created all those fortunes and wonderful old brick buildings.

I feel I've gone far afield from the Duke lacrosse scandal. I guess you could make some wild comparisons. Duke's exploitation of smokers creating a climate of destruction that yielded callous disregard for a woman's virtue. I won't do that.

You know, things have been quiet on the Duke lacrosse front, very quiet. D.A. Mike Nifong is undergoing his ethics hearing. The North Carolina Attorney General toured the crime scene, alleged. The one year anniversary passed quietly. Things have been crawling to a yawn.

So, why not give a little more background. In the wake of the scandal Duke took to trumpeting its accomplishments. It spoke of its community outreach and volunteer programs. My daughter's grade school, E.K.

Powe benefited from some of that outreach. Duke students would come to the after school programs and play learning games, read books, and generally spend time with the kids including my daughter. This was a great program and I know my daughter made some friends among the students.

Contrast this with an article I was reading in, I believe it was *The Chronicle*, that spoke about the lack of Duke professors living in this neighborhood, or any of the neighborhoods surrounding Duke for that matter. This was specifically about a lack of professor's children attending local Durham schools. The example they gave was E.K. Powe and they could not find a professor with a child there. They had to go back to a prof whose child had graduated a few years before to find a connection.

It is my supposition that many Duke professors live in Chapel Hill where the property values are higher and will remain so and will increase at a proportionately greater rate than Durham homes. It is hard to connect to a community where you have little connections. Thank you, Major Frank Burns.

All you *M*A*S*H* fans out there, you get this reference. In a related analogy, George W. Bush is Frank Burns. Think on it.

Maybe a little background on myself would be a good thing. I am writing this while looking at a calendar for the Carolina Hurricanes 2006-2007 season. There on the list of seat prices is the first row gate price of $150 a seat. As expensive as that seems to me I realize I can't even get tickets to the Upper Goal Zone at $10.29. I'm working my job as a call center representative at $10.00 an hour. More than one hour of my labor seems like a bad expense to see a hockey game.

I have this seating chart upon my cubicle's fuzzy walls because it is colorful and has a calendar. I just heard one of the bosses about how they are in eighth place. They could find themselves out of contention soon.

In some ways I feel like I could find myself out of contention soon. You see, I am flirting with bankruptcy. My finances are more than shot, they are ka-blamoed. However, I'm trying to see the positive elements of my misfortune. You know, living a simpler lifestyle with less money. Seeing every vestige of a more middle-class life dribble away little by little. I gave up my long distance recently. I'm thinking of cancelling my Internet service. If I give up my Internet then I'm thinking I may just have to cancel my phone service entirely. If it wasn't for my daughter, I probably wouldn't worry about it.

On the positive side, I am not the only person to experience hard times. I am not the first and I won't be the last. Would I have been able to experience the sublime earthy delight of field peas if I hadn't been so broke? Would I cherish my family as much, if I did not have to turn to them for solace.

How did I get myself in such dire straits? Perhaps it was thoughts that the Iraq war would not fuck up the economy as bad as it has. That combined with Bush's tax cuts has put all the money in the economy into the hands of people unwilling to spend it. Enough blaming because ultimately I am responsible. However, I'm not naive enough to think myself immune from the greater economic currents.

All these thoughts of money bring me back to a happier time. I took my daughter to Busch Gardens at Williamsburg. This was the spring of 2004. It seems so long ago now.

I was still in debt but I had a halfway decent job and things were looking up in my life. I was interviewing for a job with the Durham Symphony. It was a simple vacation but fun. How precious those times can be!

I sit here in my cubicle and look at my Chilean postcards. It makes me think of

Réunion. I would like to take a trip to this exotic Indian Ocean locale. They have some high mountains there that could be hiked. It looks like tremendous fun.

Thinking on Réunion makes me think of jet travel and global warming. As much as jets could be causing global warming would I be willing to give up my trip or take a steamer, if one could even be found to provide passage? Yet, wouldn't the island be particularly susceptible to the dangers of global warming and sea level rise?

Some pictures I saw on a website showed a motorcycle rally there. What a way to ruin paradise! Although, I suppose one race a year is not excessive. But, when you consider those cycles were flown in from France; that is an awful lot of jet fuel. So, maybe one traveler is of little consequence.

Here's a riddle. What is the best thing about Réunion? What is the worst thing about Réunion? Answer. . . the French. I must admit the thought of so many French women appeals to me. The thought is so many Frenchmen appalls. Not that I have even met very many of either variety but apparently it hasn't stopped me from prejudice. Isn't it always true that those with the least exposure with people are the most prejudiced? Of course, I know one friend who studied Chinese for years at the University then when he moved to China discovered he didn't like the people.

I better return to the scene of the crime all the way from China. So, there it stands, the Duke lacrosse house. All over the neighborhood the other houses that were sold to Duke are being refurbished. A huge dumpster full of duct hosing sat outside a house whose porch was full of hispanic-looking workers. That was across Urban Street. On my same block a house is down to particle board and awaits new siding. Landscaping is occurring and the neighborhood is mostly quiet. Duke was knocked down from the NCAA tourney in the first round so no more reason for basketball-related frivolity.

Since I'm back to the neighborhood, how about a reminiscence from those first few crazy weeks. The Duke house became the scene of a number of protests, vigils, marches, etc. One was held by a church and I went to take a look. There I met up with a neighbor to chat a bit about the insanity.

We compared notes on the previous couple of weeks, both seemingly surprised that this arose mushroom-like to sit on the landscape of our neighborhood. We talked a little of the facts of the case and how we hoped justice to be done and then he told me a story about that first week.

Before the banging of the pots and pans, before the lacrosse case had even really penetrated my consciousness there were protests at Duke lacrosse games. People whose ire had been raised. They were the early adopters in the rage game.

I vaguely recall, almost as if in a dream, news stories of protests at Duke lacrosse games. You know how watching the 11:00 news you see the smallest elements of stories as you are already half asleep. It was in this state that I saw something about Duke lacrosse game protesters.

Anyway, my neighbor had gone with his son to attend one of those protested games. On arriving at the gate a protester shoved a sign in the eleven-year-old boy's face that read, "Lacrosse Players Suck." Is it too much to ask protesters to honor the sensibilities of children?

For some reason that story made me think of the legend of Elvis in Durham. Durham is home to some legendary fat farms and apparently the King came to seek the cure. I have heard no less that three likely locations where he stayed while in town: either in someone's home on Watts Street, a trailer behind the Erwin Mills, or in the motel that is now The Opportunity Place on Chapel Hill Street. While likely, I think we all await definitive proof.

Speaking of rock-and-roll gods, Johnny Cash did a show with the Durham Symphony Orchestra at what is now the auditorium for the Durham School of the Arts. The DSO conductor Alan Nielson was telling me he said, "Hello, I'm Johnny Cash." even in rehearsal. I find that funny.

Why don't I delve into my imagined scenario of the events of that fateful eve? The accuser apparently accused three men of having gang-raped her years before the Duke event. Based on a rudimentary knowledge of statistics, the chances that one woman would be brutally gang-raped by three men in incidents years apart is simply astronomical. Thus, on a logical basis I dismiss the accuser's claim.

It seems to me there are three logical

choices for the events in relation to the accused. One, she was gang-raped twice. This is nearing impossibility in terms of odds outside of a war zone. Two, she was gang-raped once. This is still a long shot although it does occur. Three, she was never gang-raped. In terms of odds, this is near certainty.

My scenario revolves around her either being a liar or the victim of a horrific crime. But, this was from years before.

The accuser and her partner arrive at the house. The party is in progress. The guys have been drinking all day and it was this drinking that lead them to order a couple of dancers to come to their fete.

The dancers dance for a few minutes, about five or so, by their recollection.

At some point they stop. It seems there must have been a racial epithet slung by one of the Duke boys. I'm thinking something along the lines of "Dance Nigger." The dancers retreat to the bathroom either singly or together. The partner of the accuser speaks to guys outside the bathroom as I assume the guys go nuts and castigate the offender in their midst who caused the dancing to stop.

One of the accused leaves the party in a non-hurried way. He calls for a taxi and heads to Cosmic Cantina for a burrito.

The accuser removes her fingernails, either showing a detachment from events, or something akin to an aphasia. If the gang rape had occurred years before, she suffers an acute attack of post-traumatic stress disorder (PTSD) or a flashback. While there was no rape, she comes to believe something happened due to her confusion.

She comes out of the bathroom and grabs her partner. The invective spurred by the earlier epithet begins to fly. The boys fire back. One well-documented insult involves a Duke student saying to the dancers that his ancestor owned their ancestor who provided the cotton for his outfit. While I'm sure the defaming of his forefather was correct, I doubt he was wearing a shirt made from cotton over 140 years old.

This interchange continues for a few minutes and at some point one of the dancers calls the police in a manner obvious to the audience. This causes the partygoers to flee the scene in a hasty manner not wanting to deal with either Duke's or Durham's finest.

The dancers depart and reappear about half an hour later calling the police from Kroger to report an assault. When the police arrive the accuser is passed out. After being revived she is taken to the hospital for an exam.

The accuser's story changes several times but only one version makes it into the police report. For some reason the Durham PD's info does not get passed along to the Duke PD or administration.

All of these circumstances fit with an incident of PTSD. The dancer apparently was acting fine prior to the dance at the house but on her departure was stumbling and then about an hour after her initial arrival she was passed out. A drug screen shows no rape drug in her system from the event but the flashback theory explains some of her bizarre behavior.

To say that the accuser was leading a tough life involving stripping as a certitude and prostitution as a likely probability is accurate. To say that would deny her of her right to be safe in her person would be false. But to take her story at face value in ignorance of the evidence would be willful indifference to the truth.

So we return to D.A. Mike Nifong. Evidence suggests that he was involved very early in this case, although he denies a major role and implies that the Durham PD gave him this case as a complete accomplishment. Like many a prosecutor he settled on a theory of events and suspects and has refused to budge since. This unvarying quality may help D.A.'s do their jobs but it becomes a hell for the unjustly accused.

One interesting revelation in the case was that D.A. Nifong didn't interview the accused before filing charges. This would appear to be negligence of the highest order.

Finally, in the trifecta of indifference, negligence, and lastly the withholding of exculpatory evidence on his own volition, D.A. Nifong has created a nice little conviction of himself as an effective District Attorney. The last charge was brought by the revelation that D.A. Nifong did not reveal the fact that the DNA results from the dancer's body showed DNA from a number of males, none of them Duke lacrosse players.

News flash - There are some reports that today will bring an announcement from the Attorney General's office on whether they intend to continue with the prosecution of the Duke lacrosse case. Yesterday brought news that local son and daughter John and Elizabeth Edwards plan to continue his campaign for the presidency in the face of her cancer diagnosis. In reading some of the information about her prognosis the *International Herald-Tribune* said the five-year survival rate for the type of cancer she has now, the metastasizing kind, is 26%, She's a brave woman and they are a brave couple.

Another news flash - I saw John and Elizabeth Edwards on *60 Minutes* last night. They both acquitted themselves well. I feel like I should say something on a semi-related topic. It seems Katie Couric's lighting crew hates her. She was looking atrocious last night. My host father in New Zealand (I was an exchange student.) was a photographer and would always point out how badly they would light the prime minister when he was on TV. His theory was that all the folks at the publicly owned TV channel were socialists and didn't

like the National Party's Robert Muldoon. I
think Katie's makeup staff has it out for her,
too.

I'm sitting here at work. I just got back
from lunch and I am already looking towards
my next break a half hour from now. Luckily, I
can write at my job. The Internet's verboten but
slapping down these silly sentences is A-OK.
Actually, I feel like my days here are
numbered. I hope to God I get a better job
soon. That's a little prayer there. Although,
how many other jobs would give me the time
to write some stories for you.

On my break I thought about working
crappy jobs. I sit by a woman with a master's
degree. I have a master's degree. Was this a
joke on the part of the people designing this
call center's seating arrangements? Who
knows?

I've seen some people devastated by

having to take a job beneath their self-ideal.
Hell, I've been devastated a time or two,
myself. And, working all the shit jobs I have
through the years it gets discouraging at times
to not see yourself move up. Of course, with
the massive dislocations required of our post-
industrial economy, getting shafted on a semi-
regular basis is a fact of life. In fact, when I am
with someone successful often I can sense their
potent fear just below the surface that their life
could downward turn at any moment. It is
often for this reason that acquaintances desert
you when you are circling the drain. As if, poor
would rub off on them.

As I read John Kenneth Galbraith's
biography it is important to remember that the
dislocations need not have the moralistic
imprint of good and evil. Helping the working
man and preventing the chaos of widespread
uncertainty has been a boon to the corporate
world. So much so, that they rarely have a
qualm about separating masses of workers to

please their shareholders.

In my daily life I battle self-esteem issues. Why do I keep thinking that I suck for no good reason? The most recent thought was about going to a hockey game in 2001. Why would that conjure thoughts of suckiness? True, I spent money. Money I didn't have but had the credit for. And, money I was allotted for per diem expenses. We got a deal from a cop at the Passaic PD. That's where a partner and I were working. We were staying at a motel across the highway from Meadowlands Arena so it was super-convenient. But, why oh why should I think I suck for that seemingly innocuous decision.

The answer seems to be that these thoughts of suckiness are completely irrational and should be ignored. Not only ignored but combatted. Every time I have one of these thoughts I try to fight it by repeating positive affirmations. The idea is that by some point the positive affirmations will drive out the thoughts of suckiness. I think of it also as a form of negative reinforcement. Saying all those affirmations kind of sucks in its own right. So, hopefully my mind will try to avoid these damaging thoughts because the tedium of repetition will be enough incentive to help my mind to stop punishing me irrationally. In addition, the positive affirmations will be creating a better self-image for me over time.

It's funny how a good night's sleep can completely rejuvenate you. I went to sleep before nine last night. Then, was awakened by a thundershower about eleven. It was mostly heat lightning. The kind that flashes and bangs with no or little rain. Here on the Carolina Piedmont the clouds come in low and thick. In Montana I really didn't know the meaning of rolling thunder. But here the thunder rolls in a loud long low rumble. In Montana the clouds get fat and thick and bumble overhead dispensing massive thunderclaps. Here, they sweep in and attack and clap in a continuous manner.

Speaking of bumbles and comparisons and contrasts the bumblebees in North Carolina are positively huge. I have no idea how these things get off the ground. They fly around like little thimbles filling themselves with the sweet nectar of the country.

Back to my morning, after awaking refreshed — the slight rain helped drop down the masses of Carolina pollen and aided sleep, as well —I got up and did some dishes. I must have been refreshed for so mundane a task is usually pushed to the extreme back burner of my life.

News flash - All charges in the Duke lacrosse case have been dropped. They received the closest thing to a full exoneration by the North Carolina Attorney General. A.G. Roy Cooper decided not to charge the accuser for anything as he suggested she may actually believe her accusations but her story's inconsistencies were too great and in conflict with the evidence and not corroborated but contradicted by the witnesses to the event.

I just looked at the cover of the *New York Post* at www.nypost.com and they published the photo and name of the accuser. This seems particularly cruel. While it may be legal to print her picture because she is no longer technically an accuser in a sexual assault case the *N.Y. Post* should have exercised discretion and decency in allowing her to return to private life.

I went to the Duke Symphony Orchestra with my daughter last night at the Baldwin Auditorium on Duke's East Campus. It's about ½ a block from my house. There was a palpable sense of a dark cloud having been lifted, even though it was raining. The maestro Harry Davidson congratulated the orchestra and the audience saying everything was the best it had been in his eight years at Duke.

And, no doubt he was right. From the wintertime Shostakovich 5th to this spring's Schubert's 3rd the orchestra has been sounding great. Duke had been advertising its arts offering in a sensible 2nd page full page ad in *The Independent Weekly*, not hiding their information, and I have seen the audiences grow in response. They used to advertise their music programs with flyers that were haphazardly distributed. More than anything, an orchestra needs an audience.

Now, that Duke and Durham have received a reprieve, lawsuits that may be filed notwithstanding, I feel like putting this behind myself. I really don't feel like I have anything more to say on this matter, future book contracts excepted.

Afterword

More and more it seems to me this is the story of a government, Durham, and a private entity, Duke, coming together with their various police departments to target one select group of people, students. I heard on the radio the other day that student crime had dropped dramatically since the lacrosse incident. Well, the reasons it did are explained above, to reiterate: increased enforcement and the sale of student houses in my neighborhood.

However, I think we as citizens should

speak out whenever a government and a private police force decide to target one group of people. In this case it was students; and the community, myself included, remained silent.

Yesterday, former Durham District Attorney Mike Nifong was sentenced to 24 hours in jail for a conviction of contempt related to his withholding of exculpatory DNA evidence. While some of the Duke lacrosse case was the result of his rogue behavior, can we not especially fault the Duke and Durham establishments for providing the wink and nod environment for his attack on students.

Durham recently suspended its investigation into the prosecution of the students on the advice of its insurer, being wary of giving the student lawsuits ammunition. The students already having settled with Duke.

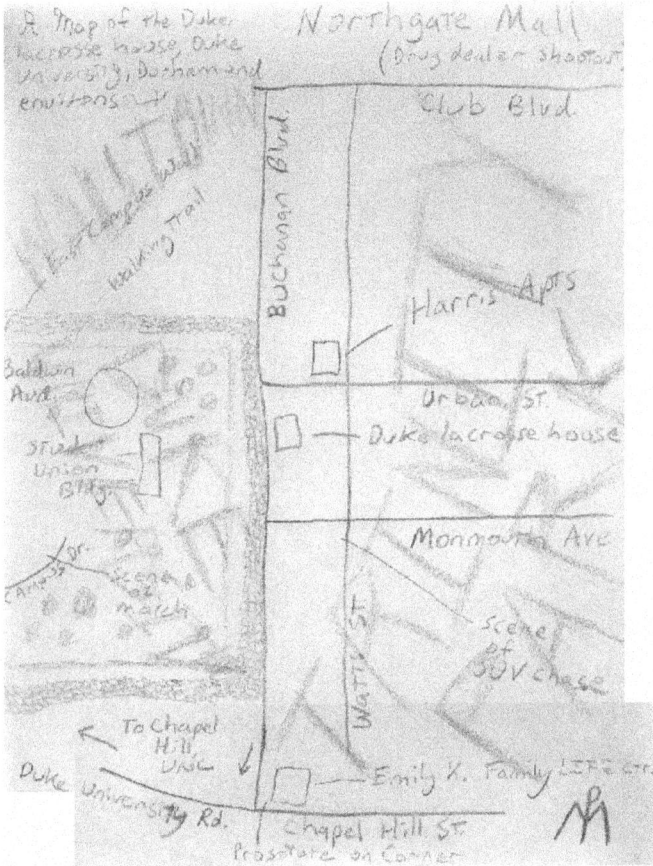

A Map of the Duke lacrosse house, Duke University, Durham and environs

Northgate Mall (Drug dealer shootout)

Club Blvd

Buchanan Blvd

East Campus Walking Trail

Harris Apts

Baldwin Ave.

Student Union Bldg

Urban St.

Duke lacrosse house

Campus Dr.

Scene of march

Monmouth Ave

Watts St.

Scene of SUV chase

To Chapel Hill UNC

Duke University Rd.

Emily K. Family Life Ctr.

Chapel Hill St.
Prostitute on Corner

www.ingramcontent.com/pod-product-compliance
Lightning Source LLC
Chambersburg PA
CBHW031952190326
41519CB00007B/768